T0194645

Finally FILLED

A Short Guide of Encouragement for those Seeking to be Endowed with the Spiritual Indwelling Presence of the Holy Ghost

DARRYL G. HOWELL

WESTBOW
PRESS®
A DIVISION OF THOMAS NELSON
& ZONDERVAN

Copyright © 2019 Darryl G. Howell.

All rights reserved. No part of this book may be used or reproduced by
any means, graphic, electronic, or mechanical, including photocopying,
recording, taping or by any information storage retrieval system
without the written permission of the author except in the case of
brief quotations embodied in critical articles and reviews.

Edited by Elite Authors
Cover design by Jason Long for Boree Unlimited
Cover Illustration by Nathan Spratt for Norma · Nathan Studios

To purchase books visit our website at
www.FinallyFilled.com

Send all correspondence to Tabholiness@gmail.com

Because of the dynamic nature of the Internet, any web addresses or
links contained in this book may have changed since publication and
may no longer be valid. The views expressed in this work are solely those
of the author and do not necessarily reflect the views of the publisher,
and the publisher hereby disclaims any responsibility for them.

Scripture taken from the King James Version of the Bible.

Holy Ghost and Holy Spirit are used interchangeably
throughout the manuscript and are one and the same.

ISBN: 978-1-9736-6555-7 (sc)
ISBN: 978-1-9736-6556-4 (hc)
ISBN: 978-1-9736-6554-0 (e)

Library of Congress Control Number: 2019907366

Print information available on the last page.

WestBow Press rev. date: 8/1/2019

WestBow Press books may be ordered through booksellers or by contacting:

WestBow Press
A Division of Thomas Nelson & Zondervan
1663 Liberty Drive
Bloomington, IN 47403
www.westbowpress.com
1 (866) 928-1240

Dedication

This book is dedicated to my loving wife, Latanya, and my two children, Darryl and Ashley, as they have been great supporters of my endeavors—both past and present.

This book is also dedicated to my parents, Lemar and Hattie Howell, and my late grandmother Mary Hatcher, as well as to my siblings, Ronald, Rhonda, and Reggie, who urged and encouraged me to write this book. Finally, it is dedicated to all the people of God who kept me encouraged until God finally filled me with the Holy Ghost.

Foreword

On May 29, 1991, the gospel was shared with Darryl G. Howell. On that same day, Darryl G. Howell confessed his sins to Jesus Christ and was saved.

A few months later, Darryl G. Howell was the recipient of another miracle when God spoke to him while he was sitting at his kitchen table. He was miraculously healed from epilepsy, which he had suffered with for thirteen long years.

On October 22, 1993, his newfound walk with Christ reached a high point when he was filled with the Holy Ghost during a Friday night church service. Six months later, Darryl G. Howell was called by God into the ministry. He is currently a pastor in a church in the urban Midwest.

In this book, you will explore the dispensational work of the Holy Ghost through the real-life experiences of the author.

You will be challenged if you question the authenticity of the Holy Ghost, and you will be convinced that God has chosen to do his work through the power of the Holy Ghost in this dispensation.

Join the author as he navigates you through his spiritual journey from salvation to Pentecost and beyond. You, too, will not want to stop until you are finally filled.

Contents

Contents

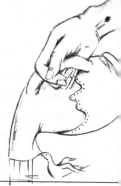

CHAPTER 1

The Unanswered Question

*Eye have not seen, nor ear heard, neither have entered into the heart
of man, the things which God have prepared for them that love him.*
—1 Cor. 2:9

"How does it feel to be endowed with God's heavenly gift?" This
is the question that I asked everyone from the beginning. I was
fascinated by the concept of being filled with the Holy Ghost, as I
had no Pentecostal church background at all. When I found out that
being filled with the Holy Ghost was scriptural and was supported
by the word of God, I became even more interested.

My wife and I had begun attending a Pentecostal church. The
people there were so excited about the Holy Ghost. When they
talked about it, you could see the glow on their faces and hear the
reverence for God in their voices.

All of this is what prompted me to start asking this question.
I believe that every single person of whom I asked this question
truly and earnestly tried to answer it to the best of his or her ability,
but each time I walked away disappointed because no one was
able to answer the question to my satisfaction. The answer that
I most frequently received was one of no explanation. I was told
by so many people that being filled with the Holy Ghost was an
experience that could not be explained.

Looking back at it now, I guess everyone answered my question
without actually answering it. The unsatisfying answers gave me

a deep thirst to investigate these things myself. All of the answers that people gave me were indeed true, but I was not satisfied with the answers that I heard.

This, in itself, illustrates that the operations of the Holy Ghost transcend the thinking and imagining of our human hearts and minds.

The concept of the unanswered question works on the believer's behalf. By not getting this question answered, it gives us the desire to experience the unknown. It gives us the desire to experience the deeper entities of God.

Most people know that when you enter into a relationship with God, you are to repent and be baptized in water. Few people, however, believe that they can be filled with the Holy Ghost. I truly believe that no one has successfully imagined how it feels to be filled with the Holy Ghost. This once again triggers this unanswered question: How does it feel to be endowed with God's heavenly gift?

Eventually, I was asking everyone I met to explain to me the experience of his or her lifetime. Because I was not satisfied with the explanations that I heard, I wanted to pursue after God even more in my quest to be endowed with His heavenly gift.

One of the most honest questions asked in New Testament Bible history was that of Nicodemus to Jesus. In the Gospel according to John 3:4, Nicodemus asked Jesus these questions: "How can a man be born when he is old? Can he enter the second time into his mother's womb, and be born?"

Although Jesus answered Nicodemus's questions, no doubt Nicodemus did not understand his answer. The reason that Nicodemus could not understand the answer that Jesus gave him is the same reason that no one could give a satisfactory answer to my question—you cannot explain that which is spiritual to someone who is not in touch with their spiritual side. My new walk with Christ had just begun, and the people at the Pentecostal church that I attended were far more spiritually mature than I was. I found myself in the same predicament as Nicodemus, seeking answers to spiritual things while I was still in the natural.

The natural man cannot understand things that are spiritual. There are many things that a man or woman in the natural will not understand until he or she is endowed with the spirit of God. Nicodemus was now faced with the reality that he needed to be spiritually awakened himself.

The best thing that can happen to people who are seeking after God is to be left with their questions unanswered. When you understand a concept too well, it leaves you with no thirst to seek the unknown or search for missing pieces. It is human nature to seek after that which a person is unsure of or that which he wants to experience.

Not having my question answered was enough to intrigue me, and it caused me to realize that I was in need of something more. It was the others' inability to answer this question that caused me to seek that which was unknown unto me.

The person who had to absorb the brunt of my questions concerning the divine indwelling of the Holy Ghost was my dear wife, Latanya. My wife had received salvation and had been converted a few years before me. Initially my wife avoided my questions and kept putting off answering them. She would say that we would discuss the topic at some other time. In fact, soon after we had the discussion, my life would change forever.

I will never forget it. We were living in that three-room apartment when I asked her again, "How does it feel to be endowed with God's heavenly gift?" This time, she opened up and began talking. She tried to answer my questions to the best of her ability. She gave me various examples and attempted to put the supernatural encounter that she had experienced into words.

We stayed up until the wee hours of the morning talking about the indwelling of the Holy Ghost. While she was not able to clearly explain every aspect of the experience, she did it justice and left me thirsting to experience this encounter for myself. Even though the question was unanswered, I felt positive about what I had learned from her, and it put me on the right track. Thanks to my wife, I was now encouraged beyond measure to seek after this experience myself. Even though the question was unanswered, it served as a starting point for my quest of spiritual enrichment. The fact that no one could answer my question is a testimony of God's awesomeness and His undefined hidden mysteries. I would not want to serve a god whom I could figure out or a god who is on the same level as me; instead, I am happy that we serve a God who surpasses our understanding.

If you, as a Christian, have only had the experience of repentance and cannot recall by physical evidence a specific place or specific time that the Holy Spirit took up residence inside of you, beware—you are selling yourself short.

God has so many blessings in store for the believer, but first we have to be honest with ourselves and realize that we need something more. As the Apostle Paul stated in 1 Corinthians 2:9, "Eye hath not seen, nor ear heard, neither have entered into the heart of man, the things which God hath prepared for them that love him." When Paul stated this, he was referring to the hidden mysteries that God has prepared for His people.

One of the greatest mysteries of our time is the fact that God would leave Heaven and come down to earth and take up residence in the soul of man. It cannot be conceived through our five senses. It is an experience of ultimate value and beauty. It is beyond your greatest imagination. It is impossible to be disappointed or let down by the Holy Ghost indwelling. Being filled with the Holy Ghost is the greatest experience that could ever happen to anyone.

Let us leave the unanswered questions to the philosophers and theologians, and let us go after God's gift. We can use the unanswered questions as motivation to seek out all that God has for us.

CHAPTER 2
The Waiting Game

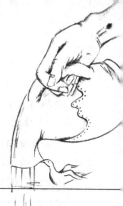

And, behold, I send the promise of my Father upon you: but tarry ye in the city of Jerusalem, until ye be endued with power from on high.
—Luke 24:49

We have heard the saying, especially when people are having a hard time waiting, "weight is what broke the bridge," but on the day of Pentecost, *wait* is what actually broke the bridge. On the day of Pentecost, God removed all of the bridges and barriers of ethnic and racial divide.

In Jesus's final discourse to His disciples before He was carried up into heaven, He told them to "tarry ye in the city of Jerusalem, until ye be endued with power from on high." - Luke 24:49

The word "tarry" means to wait. When we were growing up as children, we had a difficult time waiting on Christmas. The anxious anticipation of what we were waiting on caused time to creep by so slowly. In this fast-paced society we live in now, people do not want to wait long for anything. We have fast food, express lines in grocery stores, drive-through pickup windows, overnight mail service—all because no one is accustomed to waiting.

We tend to look at all of the negative aspects of waiting, but the positive aspects far outweigh the negative. One important positive aspect of waiting is that once you have waited and finally received what you have been waiting on, the wait causes you to be more appreciative than if you had received it right away. Waiting tends to help you value and treasure what you have received.

What if the disciples of Jesus had been filled with the Holy Ghost at the moment that they met Jesus? What do you think the outcome would have been if they did not have to wait until Pentecost? Could you imagine the confusion that would have taken place as a result of this? Do you think the disciples would have truly appreciated God's heavenly gift if they had received it right away without waiting?

When left to us, we usually do a good job of wrecking things that God has prepared for our lives. God's perfect will is worked out in our lives through waiting. Think about it—we do not pluck fruit off of a tree or dig vegetables out of the ground as soon as they become visible. Instead, we have to allow them to ripen and mature so that we can get the proper taste and nourishment from them.

When we learn to become disciplined and wait on the things that God has destined for us, we ensure that our blessing is not premature, and thus we are able to benefit from it to the fullest. Waiting can definitely work to our advantage if we exhibit patience.

THE INITIAL EXCITEMENT

Whenever we are on the verge of experiencing something new, there is an initial excitement that takes place. The disciples were excited and full of joy when Jesus breathed on them and gave them a prelude of what they were to experience at Jerusalem. "And when he had so said, he shewed unto them his hands and his side. Then were the disciples glad, when they saw the Lord. Then said Jesus to them again, peace be unto you: as my Father has sent me, even so send I you. And when he had said this, he breathed on them, and saith unto them, Receive ye the Holy Ghost."—John 20:20–22

This initial blessing that took place in the town of Bethany before Jesus was taken up into heaven no doubt left his disciples excited and filled with joy.

I must point out that when Jesus breathed on His disciples and said, "Receive ye the Holy Ghost," this was not the blessing that was intended for them in the city of Jerusalem. Let's keep in mind that Jesus breathed *on* them and not *in* them at Bethany. This was an initial sign or promise of something greater that was shortly to take place. Jesus, through breathing on them, was ensuring them that what He had promised would surely come to pass. This blessing served as a holdover until they received something greater. Experiencing God's spirit on the outside is not the same as having Him taking up residence on the inside.

Many times at the beginning of our salvation, God will allow us to experience the presence of the Holy Ghost on the outside, just as he breathed on his disciples at Bethany. Although we may experience God's presence from time to time on the outside and have a measure of the spirit at the moment of salvation, we must not mistake this blessing to be the fullness of the Holy Ghost dwelling on the inside. The purpose of this outward blessing is twofold. First, it keeps you excited and encouraged that you are on the right track to receiving something greater. Second, it gives us the strength and the willpower to resist temptations that we may encounter while we are waiting to get the Holy Ghost on the inside.

When this outward blessing begins to happen on a more consistent basis, this is a true sign that we are getting closer and closer to receiving what God has promised us.

God is favoring you when He allows you to experience these outward blessings because of your decision to accept salvation.

Please do not become complacent; the Holy Spirit that you are experiencing on the outside is the same spirit that He intends to put on the inside of you.

Remember that the best is yet to come—you have been experiencing the blessing at Bethany, but Jerusalem lies ahead.

THE TEN-DAY WAIT

After I received salvation, I was urged by many people of my new church family to start asking God for the Holy Ghost indwelling.

Luke 11:11–13 plainly states, "If a son shall ask bread of any of you that is a father, will you give him a stone? Or if he ask a fish, will he for a fish give him a serpent? Or if he shall ask an egg, will he offer him a scorpion? If ye then, being evil, know how to give good gifts unto your children: how much more shall your heavenly Father give the Holy Spirit to them who ask him?"

When the disciples returned to Jerusalem at Jesus's command, they went into an upper room, and the waiting game began.

No one was able to pinpoint the time in which God would pour out His spirit at Pentecost. When we look into our own personal lives, we can see that only God knows the time that He will endow us with the Holy Spirit. One thing is for sure: God's time is the right time.

It has been determined that the time in which the disciples went to the upper room until the day of Pentecost was ten days. This formula can be derived by taking the forty days in which Jesus was seen by His disciples (before He was taken up into heaven and subsequently commanded them to wait in Jerusalem) and subtracting forty from the fiftieth day, which was the day of Pentecost.

Keep in mind that when Jesus commanded His disciples to go to Jerusalem and wait until they were endued with power from on high, they had been following Jesus for approximately two and a half years.

I don't know whether it is false teaching or ignorance or maybe a little of both, but nowadays, new converts are being taught that they receive the Holy Ghost in His fullness at the moment of their salvation. I will not disagree that a believer receives a measure of the Holy Spirit at conversion, but remember this is not the entire package.

The disciples waited two and a half years plus an additional ten days before they received the Holy Ghost in His fullness at Pentecost. It is my personal opinion that you can pass this time in which God is seemingly prolonging the giving of His gift by learning the fundamentals of salvation. We can also spend this waiting time learning how God expects us to live and conducting ourselves as new converts, aiming to please God at any cost.

Receiving a gift without knowing the true value can cause one to not appreciate the gift. If the Holy Ghost is sought after and waited upon, the recipient appreciates the heavenly gift even more once he or she receives it.

Let us take a look at some of the activities that were taking place in the upper room during the ten-day wait. Acts 1:13–14 states, "And when they were come in, they went up into an upper room, where abode both Peter, and James, and John, and Andrew, Philip, and Thomas, Bartholomew and Matthew, James the son of Alphaeus, and Simon Zelotes, and Judas the brother of James. These all continued with one accord in prayer and supplication, with the women, and Mary the mother of Jesus, and with his brethren."

The two key activities were prayer and supplication. If the disciples prayed and supplicated for ten days straight, surely we can do the same in the small time allotments we have set aside in our worship services.

The ten days of prayer and supplication allowed everyone who was present in the upper room to become attuned and in the right mind-set to receive the gift of the Holy Ghost.

More people have received the Holy Ghost in these types of services—where the people waited and supplicated before the Lord—than in any other place. If you have never witnessed or experienced these types of services or meetings, do not be discouraged. God is able to fill you with the Holy Ghost wherever you are. God has always made the unavailable available for those who seek Him earnestly.

This ten-day wait also served as a tool to clear the minds of the disciples so that they could focus on the promise for which Jesus had sent them there. It is easier to focus on Jesus when we keep our minds on Him continually through praises.

Luke 24:52–53 states the following: "And they worshipped him, and returned to Jerusalem with great joy: And were continually in the temple praising and blessing God. Amen."

I presume that the disciples who were present in the upper room spent this time emptying themselves and praising and blessing God for several days before they were able to get on one accord.

Acts 2:1 states, "And when the day of Pentecost was fully come, they were all with one accord in one place." We are not truly ready to receive God's gift until we get to the place where being filled with the heavenly gift of the Holy Ghost becomes first and foremost in our life. We have to get on one accord with those around us, and if we are alone, we have to focus our minds on what Jesus has in store for us.

WAITING EXEMPLIFIES WORTHINESS

The best way for us to prove to God that we are worthy of His gift is through our willingness to wait. Although we are undeserving of God's gift, waiting proves to God that we trust His discretion in giving us His heavenly gift. Our willingness to wait causes our waiting to be transformed into worthiness.

Waiting proves to God that we have changed our will to His will. Our will would have us to receive the heavenly gift right away and possibly take God's gift and use it for our own selfish desires.

Waiting demonstrates that the receiving of God's gift is not predicated upon who we are—our race, social status, financial stability or instability—but is predicated upon the will of God and what He desires to accomplish in our lives.

Waiting also gives us time to go on a soul search. We should never feel that we are so worthy of God's gift that we can demand God to let us receive it right away.

Instead, waiting gives us the time to examine ourselves and at the same time ask God to show us ourselves so that we may correct the things in our lives that do not please God.

Waiting is a humbling experience. We are already on the wrong track if we feel that we can demand God's heavenly gift of the Holy Ghost without repenting of our sins and asking God to clean our inward man so that the Holy Ghost will be pleased to dwell on the inside. This includes cleansing one's self from indulgences in drugs, alcohol, tobacco, fornication, pornography, evil communication, and all other worldly lust. 1 Corinthians 6:19 says, "Know ye not that your body is the temple of the Holy Ghost which is in you, which ye have of God, and ye are not your own?"

After repentance, when we make a vow to live a life free from sin, we are inviting the Holy Ghost to come in and take up residence in our fleshly house. Cleaning up our fleshly house indicates to God that we want the Holy Ghost to abide inside of us, no matter how long we have to wait.

If you have not yet been filled with the Holy Ghost, don't be discouraged; it is just time for you to play the waiting game.

CHAPTER 3

The Most Important Gift

If ye then, being evil, know how to give good gifts unto
your children: how much more shall your heavenly
Father give the Holy Spirit to them that ask him?
—Luke 11:13

Gifts are something that we all enjoy receiving. If you want to brighten up a person's day, just give them a gift, and their expressions will say it all. The greatest gift that God gave to the world was His own son, Jesus Christ, but the most important gift that God gave to the church in this age was the gift of the Holy Ghost.

In the eleventh chapter of Luke, the name "Holy Spirit" is used instead of the name "Holy Ghost." In the King James Version, "Ghost" occurs ninety times, while "Spirit" occurs seven times. Don't be confused—the Holy Ghost and Holy Spirit are one and the same.

In this particular chapter, the disciples came to Jesus with a request to teach them how to pray as John taught his disciples. One of the most remarkable things about our savior Jesus Christ is that He already knows whether you need what you are requesting. If you are truly in need, He knows how to make provision for you and also His church.

In the beginning of the chapter, the topic of discussion is prayer, but by the end of the chapter, the topic of discussion changes to the

Holy Spirit. At first glimpse, it may seem that prayer has nothing to do with the Holy Spirit, but upon a second glimpse, it is clear that prayer has everything to do with the Holy Spirit. Jesus not only taught his disciples how to pray; He also taught them what the focus of their prayers should be on.

In the eleventh chapter of Luke, Jesus not only taught them the dynamics of prayer; he also taught them the most important thing that they should be praying for. Jesus, knowing what they stood in need of before they asked, deflected their desires off of carnal things to the gift that was most important for their souls.

We have to keep in mind that the disciples left all in order to follow Jesus, and there were definitely some times when things got a little tight—or, for lack of a better word, a lot tight. The disciples depended on Jesus to meet every one of their everyday needs, and no doubt the disciples who were small in faith were uncertain about the future.

Jesus takes this moment of uncertainty to teach his disciples about prayer. Jesus used the first five verses of the eleventh chapter of Luke to instruct them in the specifics of prayer, but keep in mind that the ultimate goal of prayer that Jesus was trying to get them to achieve was in verse 13.

"Our Father": "Our Father" signifies a personal relationship between God and the believer. If a believer can get on his knees and address God as "Our Father," this denotes that the believer is in good standing with God.

"Which art in heaven": When the believer makes this affirmation, he or she is displaying his or her faith in God by stating his or her belief that He exists. It also taught the disciples that they did not serve a god who was limited or who could be

contained in the confines of the earth but whose dwelling place was in the heavens.

"Hollowed be Thy name": This signifies worship. God is looking for true worshippers. Jesus wanted his disciples—along with us—to revere the name of God.

"Thy kingdom come": This signifies expectation. Jesus taught His disciples that they should pray and live their life expecting Jesus to return at any moment.

"Thy will be done, as in heaven, so in earth": This signifies submission. God's will is done in heaven, but also, our lives that we live here on earth should be subject to what God wants.

"Give us this day our daily bread": This signifies trust. Jesus taught the disciples that God would meet their everyday needs, both natural and spiritual.

"Forgive us of our sins": This signifies confession. This taught the disciples that they should forgive men of their sins just as the Father forgave them of their sins.

"Lead us not into temptation but deliver us from evil": This signifies divine guidance. This taught the disciples that God cannot be tempted with evil, nor does He tempt us. Instead, he will readily steer us around Satan's traps.

In Jesus's teaching on the model prayer in verses 2 through 4, we can discover six principles that must be in place before we are ready to receive what God has for us in verse 13: our relationship with God, faith, worship, expectation, submission, and confession.

Jesus, in His divine wisdom, knew that the believer could not receive the gift of the Holy Spirit until these six principles were set in place. These natural requests that Jesus instructed His disciples to pray for led them right into the six spiritual principles needed to obtain the ultimate goal stated in verse 13.

Luke 11:13 states, "If ye then, being evil, know how to give good gifts unto your children: how much more shall your heavenly Father give the Holy Spirit to them that ask him?" Jesus wanted his disciples to know that God cared about and would supply their everyday needs. More importantly, He wanted them to know that there is one spiritual desire that should take precedent over their natural needs: the gift of the Holy Spirit.

Jesus did not condemn them for praying for natural things; instead, he showed them that their prayers should be prioritized. Matt 6:33 states, "But seek ye first the kingdom of God, and his righteousness; and all these things shall be added unto you."

Jesus wanted them to know if they sought first that which was spiritual (the kingdom of God), the natural (these things) would be added. One may ask, what is Jesus's interpretation of the kingdom of God? If we take into consideration what the Apostle Paul writes, we may come to the conclusion that Jesus interprets the kingdom of God to be the Holy Spirit and all that pertains to it.

In Romans 14:17, Paul states, "For the kingdom of God is not meat and drink; but righteousness, and peace, and joy in the Holy Ghost." The Apostle Paul differentiates the natural (meat and drink) from the spiritual (righteousness, peace, and joy in the Holy Ghost).

The fact that peace and joy are fruit of the spirit (according to Galatians 5) further strengthens this claim. One may now ask, where does righteousness come in?

If we look at John 16:8, Jesus states, "And when he [the Holy

Spirit] is come, he will reprove the world of sin and of righteousness." Thus, it is the job of the Holy Spirit to do the following three things: make righteousness known to the world, prove to the world that Jesus was righteous, and execute righteousness through every believer.

We can now conclude that righteousness is a ministry of the Holy Spirit and cannot deny that Jesus is referring to the Holy Spirit and all that pertains to Him when He mentions righteousness or the kingdom of God.

With that said, let's look at the request of one of Jesus's disciples, which prompted this discourse that Jesus gave on prayer. In Luke 11:1, one of his disciples made a request as he said, "Lord, teach us to pray, as John also taught his disciples."

Jesus took this precious opportunity to teach his disciples not only what they should be praying for but also how to prioritize their prayers and not allow the natural needs of everyday life to overshadow their need for the most important gift of all, the gift of the Holy Spirit.

What was it about John's disciples' prayer life that caught the attention of this disciple of Jesus? If we just take a quick glimpse at the life of John the Baptist, we will see that John, for the most part, led a simple lifestyle. We can determine that John's simple lifestyle enabled him not to become entangled with the cares of the world. If we take into consideration that every leader will pass on the attributes that they possess to their followers, it would be fair to speculate that John taught his disciples how to pray and what things to pray for.

In conjunction with his God-given assignment to preach repentance and to prepare the way of the Lord, we can gain much insight on what John was called to do and who called him to do it. We can also see the values that he taught his disciples as they related to his own calling. In reference to God, John states in John 1:33, "And I knew him not: but he that sent me to baptize with water, the same said unto me, Upon whom thou shalt see the Spirit descending, and remaining on him, the same is he which baptizeth with the Holy Ghost."

Undoubtedly, it was God who sent John to baptize, preach repentance, and prepare the way for the Savior. To ensure that there was no doubt in John's mind in whom he was preparing the way for, God told John to look for a sign that he would not be able to deny.

The sign that God told John to look for was the Holy Spirit descending upon an individual in the form of a dove. That same individual in whom the dove remained upon would be the same who would baptize others with the Holy Ghost. Of course, the individual to whom God was referring was none other than Jesus Christ.

When speaking of the Savior, it is noteworthy that when God gave John the instructions for his ministry, He did not say, "Upon whom thou shalt see the Spirit descending, the same is he which will heal the sick" or "the same is he which will raise the dead." Instead, God stated that which was most important—the fact that Jesus would endow believers with the Holy Ghost.

John the Baptist, in his own respect, had a great ministry that had its place and purpose, but John also knew that he was making the way for someone with an even greater God-given ministry. In Matthew 3:11, John states, "I indeed baptize you with water unto repentance: but he that cometh after me is mightier than I, whose shoes I am not worthy to bear: he shall baptize you with the Holy Ghost, and with fire."

Because God did not mention the many other attributes that Jesus would possess but instead chose to mention the most important attribute—the attribute of the Holy Spirit—we can only assume that John passed on the importance of this ministry to his disciples. So it would be safe to say that John trained and instructed his disciples to pray concerning the ministry of the Holy Spirit as John himself had been endowed with the Holy Spirit from the womb. Luke 1:15 states, "He shall be great in the sight of the Lord, and shall drink neither wine nor strong drink; and he shall be filled with the Holy Ghost, even from his mother's womb." So then it would be safe to speculate that it was the pre-Pentecostal prayers concerning the Holy Spirit that caught the attention of Jesus's disciples.

Jesus wasted no time in honoring his disciples' request by addressing what was on his mind and what is on most of our minds when we pray—the carnal desires of everyday life. Let's face it: praying is not easy. When we pray, we tend to allow our natural needs to come in and overshadow our spiritual needs. Jesus knew that we, along with the disciples who came to Him with this request, would face this same obstacle that we face.

In chapter 11 of Luke, Jesus does not teach against material things and earthly needs, but instead He teaches us how to put these things in the right perspective, giving first priority to things that are spiritual. In verses 5 through 8, after Jesus gives his discourse on the model prayer, He then resorts to the use of parables to further strengthen His claim of the importance of the believer receiving the gift of the Holy Spirit.

In this particular parable, there are two main characters: the man in the bed and the friend who came to him at midnight. In this parable, the man in the bed represents God. The friend who came to him at midnight represents the believer. The bread represents the Holy Spirit. Notice that the friend did not want the bread for himself but for the person who came to him on his journey. Luke 11:6 says, "For a friend of mine in his journey has come to me, and I have nothing to set before him."

This friend who came to him represents the people whom we meet and come in contact with on a day-to-day basis. These are the people whom we encounter every day in our jobs, on the street, or anywhere else we may go. The Holy Spirit is not given to us for ourselves; rather, it is given to us to share with others. How many times have people come to us and we were unable to minister unto them because we didn't have any bread? How many of us are trying to do the work of the Lord when we don't have any bread? We must ask God to give us the bread of the Holy Spirit so that we can share with those who are in need. The dope pusher, the drug addict, the prostitute, the gangster, and the person locked up in jail need some of our bread.

The man in the bed, which represents God, was tucked in for the night, and his children were in bed with him. He first refused to get out of bed to meet the need of his friend, but because of his friend's importunity, as stated in verse 8, the man in the bed got up and gave his friend as many loaves as he needed.

The word "importunity" is defined as unwavering perseverance rising to the point of shamelessness. This man did not care what time of night it was when he knocked on the door. He came at midnight and was not ashamed because he was in desperate need.

When we are seeking to be filled with the Holy Ghost, we can't wait for business hours to ask God for what we need. We can't wait for a church to schedule a revival to ask God for what we need. When we need something from God, we need it right now—in a hurry. We have to be persistent and keep knocking on the door until God gets out of the bed and gives us what we need.

This man's importunity caused the man in the bed to rise and not just give him one loaf. Instead, he gave him as many loaves as he needed. These multiple loaves may very well represent the gifts of the Holy Spirit that are available to every believer who asks for them.

In verses 9 and 10, Jesus now tells us the actions we should take when seeking to be endowed with the Holy Spirit. Jesus states in Luke 11:9, "Ask, and it shall be given you; seek, and ye shall find; knock, and it shall be opened unto you." Asking, knocking, and seeking are all actions that are necessary if one wants to be endowed with the Holy Spirit.

Jesus does not put any limitation on who can receive the gift of the Holy Ghost. In verse 10, He says, "For every one that asketh receiveth; and he that seeketh findeth; and to him that knocketh it shall be opened." This means that anyone who comes into the knowledge of Jesus Christ—regardless of race, creed, or color—is eligible to partake of and receive this heavenly gift.

In verses 11 and 12, Jesus makes known the fact that our Father in heaven is like a natural father and will not give his children things that will harm them. He makes mention in these verses of serpents, scorpions, and stones, along with fish, eggs, and bread. Now, if your natural father can differentiate which of these things are good and which are bad, then your heavenly Father knows that the Holy Spirit is good for you and wants you to have it.

In conclusion, in verse 13, Jesus states, "If ye then, being evil, know how to give good gifts unto your children: how much more shall your heavenly Father give the Holy Spirit to them who ask him."

As we recap, we can see that Jesus has taught us how to prioritize, putting our spiritual needs before our natural needs. He uses a parable to show us that if we are persistent in prayer, we can get anything we need from God as long as it is in His will.

He shows us that the simple actions of asking, knocking, and seeking are necessary if we expect God to respond to our desires and prayer requests. He proves to us that God is able to determine what is good for us and what we need, even when we don't know what is good for ourselves.

Now with this formula set in place, let's not waste time asking God for carnal or natural things that many of us have the power to attain ourselves. Instead, let us ask God for the most important gift, which we cannot give ourselves—the gift of the Holy Spirit.

CHAPTER 4

Shoes Without Tongues

And they were all filled with the Holy Ghost, and began to speak
with other tongues, as the Spirit gave them utterance.
—Acts 2:4

Every type of shoe that you see—whether it's a dress shoe, a gym shoe, or a slip-on—has something in common with all others: it comes with a tongue.

The tongue of the shoe is designed to give support to the top of the foot while walking or running so that the foot will not come out of the shoe and so that you can sustain maximum balance. Could you imagine doing any type of physical activity wearing shoes without tongues? In the same way that the tongue of the shoe supports the foot, speaking in an unknown tongue is the believer's support and confirmation that he or she has been filled with the Holy Ghost.

I don't wish to make and argument as to when or how much a believer should speak in tongues, nor do I wish to discuss the use of tongues as a spiritual gift. Rather, I wish to discuss the importance of tongues as the initial evidence of one who has been filled with the Holy Ghost.

There is a movement going on now all across the world—one that has probably been going on for some time now—of people who say they have been filled with the Holy Ghost but who do not speak in tongues and therefore provide no evidence of being filled with the Holy Ghost. Articles have been written in some of the most noteworthy gospel magazines of our day stating that there are millions of people across the world claiming to have received the Holy Ghost without speaking in tongues. I would not go as far as to say that a person who has not spoken in tongues is not saved or is not endowed with the Holy Spirit, but I will say that it is important for us to have conformation that the Holy Ghost is residing inside of us.

✟

An inventory analyst from Merrillville, Indiana, writes the following:

I started seeking after the Holy Spirit in July 2005 at a youth revival. The woman evangelist called everyone up and had everyone repent and call on Jesus. In November of 2006, I stopped asking God for the Holy Spirit and began thanking Him for the Holy Spirit. I continued to fast and pray and seek Him even more. On January 5, 2007, during an all-night prayer meeting, I got in the prayer line and told the Lord that I did not want to leave until I received the fullness of the Holy Spirit. I told Him that I wanted the Holy Spirit more than anything in the world. I asked the Lord to search my heart and to move every mountain out of my way. As I moved up in the line, I began to feel sharp pains in my stomach, but I continued to praise the Lord. By the time I got to the front of the line, all the pains were gone. I lifted my hands up and began to praise God. At that point I could hear everyone around me praising God. As I was praising God, my tongue was moving on its own, and I began speaking in an unknown tongue.

Just as the tongue is the supporting component of the shoe for the foot, speaking in tongues is your support and confirmation that you have received the Holy Ghost.

Once again, by no means am I stating that a person who has not spoken in tongues is not saved. Keep in mind that the Holy Ghost is the one who convicts or convinces a sinner that he or she needs to be saved. So it is probable that a person at salvation has a measure of the Spirit and thus is compelled to live a life that is Christ-like.

Notice that John 20:23 did not state that He breathed in them, but instead "He breathed on them." The disciples were full of joy from their outward blessing that they experienced at Bethany, but this was just enough to whet their appetites in anticipation of what was to happen when they made it to Jerusalem. Jesus then told them in Luke 24:49, "And, behold, I send the promise of my Father upon you: but tarry ye in the city of Jerusalem, until ye be endued with power from on high." Jesus wanted His disciples to not only receive the outward blessing, but he had also ordained for them to receive an inward filling in the upper room at Pentecost.

Acts 2:4 states, "And they were all filled with the Holy Ghost, and began to speak with other tongues, as the Spirit gave them utterance." Without the beautiful God-given sign of speaking in tongues, how else will the believer and those around him or her be confident that the speaker was been endowed with God's heavenly gift?

✞

A retired receiving clerk from Lansing, Illinois, writes, "I started seeking the Holy Spirit after hearing beautiful stories from people who had received the Holy Spirit. After many disappointments, I became more determined than ever to receive the Holy Spirit. In a revival that I attended while at the altar, I saw a great light, and the light became brilliant, and everything around me was not. I was connected to this brilliant light, and I began to speak in tongues. I am not sure of the time, but a spirit of worship and thanksgiving followed. I thank God for the gift of the Holy Spirit."

When the disciples were filled with the Holy Ghost on the day of Pentecost, there were devout Jews at Jerusalem in town for the feast. When these Jews came together, they witnessed the awesome power of God. After receiving the Holy Ghost, the Holy Ghost then gave them the ability to speak in a variety of unknown tongues. Some of the Jews who witnessed this great outpouring from Heaven thought that those who were speaking in tongues were drunk. This initial sign of speaking in tongues not only served as a sign to the Jews who were witnessing this event—it also served as a much-needed sign to the 120 people in the upper room who received the gift of the Holy Ghost.

The Holy Ghost still works the same today and will be a witness to the people who are around you when you receive Him. God always leaves witnesses to confirm His work. Therefore, speaking in tongues serves as support to the believer and to his or her peers as indisputable evidence that one has received the gift of the Holy Ghost.

Speaking in tongues can also be classified as a spillover effect of being filled with the Holy Ghost. That is why it is sometimes called the baptism in the Holy Ghost because when a person is baptized, he or she is fully engulfed or endowed with the Holy Spirit. If you baptize or fully engulf a glass in water, when it comes back up, it is impossible for some of the water not to be in the inside of the glass. When the believer speaks in an unknown tongue as the initial sign, the unknown tongue expresses to others that the believer has been filled with the Holy Ghost and that He has taken up residence on the inside of that individual.

The baptism or spillover effect, accompanied with speaking in tongues, is the first inward sign that a believer experiences. The Holy Ghost will later manifest Himself to the believer through other outward and inward signs, providing witnessing power—the ability to spread the word about Jesus—and inward comfort—peace on the inside when things are in turmoil on the outside. Speaking in an unknown tongue serves as a testimony to the recipient that he or she has received the gift of the Holy Spirit. While it is important that others know that you have received the gift of the Holy Spirit, nothing is more important than your own knowledge that you have been blessed with it.

An operations supervisor from Gary, Indiana, writes the following:

In the year 2001, I thought I was already filled with the Holy Ghost. I was saved but realized I was missing something. I witnessed many times people at the altar speaking in tongues. I then thought to myself, *I need the Holy Spirit and want to receive it just the way the apostles did on the day of Pentecost.* When I did not receive the Holy Spirit, I became discouraged and felt that God had abandoned me. I was fasting, praying, and reading my Bible and was being encouraged by many to hold on and to stay with God. I attended a church service where the pastor called for those who wanted to be filled with the Holy Spirit to come to the altar. I immediately went up to the front of the line. The pastor prayed for me and then laid his hands on my chest, and I felt a warm feeling in my body. I was then knocked to the ground. I began to feel even warmer, and then it felt as if my stomach were boiling. I began to speak in tongues. After this, I was out of myself, and the rest of my experience was told to me by those who had witnessed it. God is truly a good God, and I would not trade the Holy Spirit for anything in this world. All praises and glory be to God.

I want to encourage the believer not to leave the altar until he or she is fully convinced that he or she has been filled with the Holy Ghost. When a believer speaks in an unknown tongue as the Holy Spirit gives utterance, this is further proof that the Holy Ghost is dwelling on the inside of him or her.

Furthermore, when you experience the Holy Ghost speaking out of you and you know that it is not you speaking of your own accord, this serves as concrete evidence that the Holy Ghost has taken up residency inside of you. So don't settle for an experience in which you are asked to speak in an unknown tongue of your own accord or by your own utterance. It is the Holy Ghost who speaks out of you and gives the utterance for you to speak in an unknown tongue. When the Holy Ghost speaks out of you in an unknown tongue, you have all the support you need to feel confident that you are adequately equipped to do the work of the Lord. If you leave the altar before having this experience, you will be like the foot that slips out of the shoe when engaged in activity because there was no tongue for support.

You will lack the proper support that you need, and you won't be able to gain footing in order to do the work of the Lord. So please don't be in a hurry and leave the altar before the Holy Ghost dwells in you. If you leave the altar before you have this experience, it will be like purchasing something from the store and not getting a receipt. Without a receipt, there is really no proof that you made a purchase. If you leave the altar without speaking in tongues, there is really no proof that you have received the Holy Ghost.

Therefore, it is truly important to keep on seeking God until He fills you with the Holy Spirit and allows you to speak in an unknown tongue as the Holy Spirit gives utterance. If you refuse to leave the altar and instead wait until you are filled, this will be the experience of a lifetime—one that no one will be able to take away from you.

Do you remember the day that you accepted Christ into your life? Do you remember the day that you were baptized in water? Although these are noteworthy days, the day that you are filled with the Holy Ghost and speak in an unknown tongue as initial evidence will equal—if not surpass—the other days. The power of the Holy Ghost is just that awesome.

Another argument that has been stated by many is that speaking in tongues was only for the apostles. If this is true, we as gentiles would be in trouble. No doubt the Apostle Peter was of this same mind, but God taught the Apostle Peter that the Holy Spirit was ordained to be given to the gentiles as well as the Jews.

The beautiful account of how God poured out the Holy Ghost upon the gentiles is found in Acts 10:44–46: "While Peter yet spake these words, the Holy Ghost fell on all them which heard the word. And they of the circumcision which believed were astonished, as many as came with Peter, because that on the gentiles also was poured out the gift of the Holy Ghost. For they heard them speak with tongues, and magnify God." Once again, the speaking in tongues served as the initial sign to the Jews that the gentiles also had received the Holy Ghost, and it also served as a sign to the gentiles themselves that they had received the Holy Ghost, and as a result, they magnified God.

The tongues play a significant role in identifying those who have received the Holy Ghost. These gentiles were now able to rest in the fact that the same experience that had happened to the Jews at Pentecost also happened to them. More importantly, the Holy Ghost came with the same sign of speaking in tongues. Without the evidence of speaking in tongues, Peter would not have been able to give his testimony that is found in Acts 11:15–17: "And as I began to speak, the Holy Ghost fell on them, as on us at the beginning. Then remembered I the word of the Lord, how that He said, John indeed baptized with water; but ye shall be baptized with the Holy Ghost. Forasmuch then as God gave them the like gift as He did unto us, who believed on the Lord Jesus Christ; what was I, that I could withstand God?"

Once again, speaking in tongues is the initial sign from God that one has received the gift of the Holy Spirit. This is the way that God has ordained it and intended it to be. When we try to bypass that way and come up with another way, we are guilty of withstanding God.

Let's make up our minds that we want to do it God's way by allowing ourselves to use speaking in tongues as evidence of the Holy Ghost taking up residence within us. God has work for every believer to do, but the believer must first be equipped to do the work. The Holy Ghost is the equipment that we need to do any work that God calls us to do.

Shoes always come with tongues. If you have already made the claim that you have received the Holy Ghost and have not yet spoken in tongues, you are in essence selling yourself short.

Therefore, you lack the necessary support that you need to engage in kingdom building. If you find yourself in this scenario, don't be afraid to humble yourself and start over again. It is better to start over and get it right than to continue on and never get it right. If you do go back and seek God—if you do it the right way—you will never be accused of wearing shoes without tongues.

CHAPTER 5

The Billion-Dollar A$pect

But we have this treasure in earthen vessels, that the
excellency of the power may be of God, and not of us.
—2 Cor. 4:7

If someone offered me a billion dollars in exchange for the experience I had on a Friday night in October 1993, I would not even have to think about it or ponder over it. I would turn down the billion dollars at the drop of a hat—or even more quickly, in the blink of an eye. There is not enough money in the world that would make it worth trading in the experience that happened to me on that particular night.

When I was filled with the Holy Ghost, someone asked me, how did the experience feel? The experience was so out of the ordinary that I had trouble finding the right words to explain it. I did not want to do the Holy Ghost an injustice by not being able to explain the experience adequately, so when asked the question, I simply replied, receiving the gift of the Holy Ghost is such an awesome experience that if someone offered you a billion dollars in exchange for the experience you just encountered, you—without any question or hesitation—would turn it down. There is no amount of money in the world that could equal or take the place of that experience. There are some things that God has ordained for His people that all of the money of the world cannot buy, and the Holy Ghost is definitely one of them.

When God baptizes a believer with the Holy Ghost, He is leaving the believer with an inheritance, much in the way that we try to leave an inheritance behind for our children. Naturally, a billion dollars would certainly be an adequate amount of money to leave behind for our children in order to meet all of their needs. Our Father in heaven leaves us, His children, the gift of the Holy Ghost in order to meet all of our needs while we are here on earth.

Our heavenly Father not only meets our everyday needs, but He has also left us with an inheritance that we cannot put a price tag on—an inheritance that we can take with us into eternal life.

NATURAL vs. SPIRITUAL / HAPPINESS vs. JOY

Although a billion dollars would be great to have and would make life much easier, a billion dollars would do little—if anything—for us spiritually.

Money brings along with it a feeling of happiness. We are happy at the end of the week when we get our paycheck, but as soon as we pay a few bills and the money is spent, the happiness goes away. Even for those who are fortunate enough to have an overflow in their bank accounts and who can then invest and buy real estate, the happiness that this money brings is still short-lived.

Money cannot bring us true happiness because money deals with the natural man, and it does little or nothing for the spiritual man. The money that brings us happiness naturally could never bring us joy spiritually.

There is a void or an empty space in man's soul that can only be filled or satisfied with spiritual things. Contrary to popular belief, a billion dollars would not be enough money to fill that void. That is one of the problems that we face today, as people attempt to fill that spiritual void with money or other things that are material.

On the other hand, when God fills a believer with the Holy Ghost, He is not only giving you something that money can't buy; God is also satisfying the spiritual void in your soul. When God endows a believer with the Holy Ghost, He is essentially leaving an eternal inheritance that cannot be taken away. A natural inheritance that is corruptible cannot be taken with us into eternal life.

The Holy Ghost brings along with it joy. Happiness comes from the outside, but joy resonates from the inside. The Holy Ghost supplies the believer with joy on the inside that surpasses any amount of happiness that a billion dollars could bring. It is noteworthy that joy, which resonates on the inside as a result of being filled with the Holy Ghost, is able to sustain us through tough times when we don't have any money, but money is unable to sustain us in times when we don't have any joy.

"THY MONEY PERISHES WITH THEE"

In Acts, we find the following story:

But there was a certain man, called Simon, which beforetime in the same city used sorcery, and bewitched the people of Samaria, giving out that himself was some great one: To whom they all gave heed, from the least to the greatest, saying, This man is the great power of God...And when Simon saw that through laying on of the apostles' hands the Holy Ghost was given, he offered them money, saying, Give me also this power, that on whomsoever I lay hands, he may receive the Holy Ghost. But Peter said unto him, Thy money perish with thee, because thou has thought that the gift of God may be purchased with money. (Acts 8:9–10 and 18–20)

There is no greater story that depicts the superiority of the Holy Ghost over money than the story of Simon the sorcerer. Simon was a man who had a significant impact on the city of Samaria. The city looked up to him; they saw him as a great man who had the power of God. The people did not know that Simon used witchcraft in order to deceive the people into thinking he was operating by the power of God.

When Peter and John came to town, operating in the true power of God, Simon and his sorcery was exposed. Furthermore, once Simon saw the true power of God operating through Phillip, Peter, and John, he repented. Acts 8:13 says, "Then Simon himself believed also: and when he was baptized, he continued with Phillip, and wondered, beholding the miracles and signs which were done."

Simon was greatly amazed when he saw the power of God working through Phillip, Peter, and John, but the miracle that knocked him off of his feet was when he saw the believers in Samaria receive the Holy Ghost by the laying on of hands. Simon allowed the greatest opportunity of his lifetime to slip through his fingertips. Instead of asking the apostles to lay hands on him so that he might receive the Holy Ghost, he instead requested in Acts 8:19, "Give me also this power, that on whosoever I lay hands, he may receive the Holy Ghost."

Instead of desiring the Holy Ghost for spiritual renewal, Simon was more concerned with how he could use the gift of God in order to bring himself money. Peter sensed Simon's ungodly agenda and said, as Acts 8:20 reveals, "Thy money perish with thee, because thou has thought that the gift of God may be purchased with money."

That is the problem with many of our churches today. Instead of putting their focus on the Holy Ghost, which is eternal, many churches are turning their focus toward money, which is temporal and will perish.

Don't get me wrong—money is a great necessity in the church, but we have to keep things in the proper perspective. There is nothing wrong with having money and wealth—it has its place. God wants His people to prosper and be well taken care of. The Apostle John writes in 3 John 2, "Beloved, I wish above all things that thou mayest prosper and be in health, even as thy soul prospereth."

We cannot afford to put the cart before the horse. All the money in the world will not do us any good if we lose our eternal soul. Mark 8:36 states, "For what shall it profit a man, if he shall gain the whole world, and lose his own soul."

Along with our natural prosperity, God has also laid out a

design for our soul to prosper. God has given us the gift of the Holy Ghost in order to prosper our souls.

If we use the illustration of the church being a car with a front and rear seat, we could say that many churches have allowed the gospel of prosperity to take the front seat, while the Holy Spirit is riding in the back. In many churches, the gospel of prosperity has become the main message. In some cases, these churches have bewitched believers into thinking that if they don't have any money, they are not in the will of God. If the church as a whole would make the Holy Ghost its first priority for believers, it would be clear to believers that even if they never get any money, they could never lose their souls.

THE MISSIONARY AND ME

There was a great missionary at my former church who played a significant role in helping me to realize the importance of receiving the Holy Ghost as opposed to attaining money.

In the summer of 1992, the Lord blessed my family and I with our first house. Like any other family who moves into their first home, we wanted to get some things and start fixing it up. This came at a time when my spiritual walk with God was on the rise. I had been seeking God and asking Him to fill me with the gift of the Holy Ghost since my conversion in 1991.

At that particular time, I had a full-time job, but in the summer of 1993, I took on a second job on the weekends driving a coach bus in order to get some of the things we wanted for the house. This second job caused me to miss some of the Sunday services at the church that I had formally attended. This did not sit well with the missionary.

My first thoughts were that the missionary was against me working a second job and did not want me to obtain some of the things that I wanted for our new house. Looking back at it all now, I did not know that the missionary was not against me working a second job, but she was against me making my second job my first priority. I did not see it then, but the missionary knew that the second job was becoming my main focus, and the Holy Ghost was slipping into the background.

One Sunday that I was actually in church, the missionary confronted me. She had witnessed the spiritual progress that God was allowing me to make, and she did not want my desire to receive the Holy Ghost to get lost or sidetracked while I worked this second job. These were her words: "I noticed that you have been missing a lot of church lately. I don't have anything against you working a second job. I just don't want to see you get sidetracked after you have come such a long way. I don't want to see these distractions cause you to lose the ground that you have gained in your relationship with God."

The missionary knew that I was not mature enough in my newfound walk with Christ to juggle a second job and stay focused enough to attain what God had ordained for my life. Our adversary, Satan, will use any distraction to try to keep you from receiving what God has in store for you.

I didn't really agree with the missionary but I respected her, so I heeded her words. Shortly after, one Friday night, I had just gotten off work, and I came home, ate, showered, and went to bed. Shortly after I lay down, I got a call from the bus company, which was my weekend job, to go on a 350-mile trip. This trip was to leave on Friday night and return home Sunday morning about 10:00 a.m. There would not be enough time to prepare for church and make it there in time. Once again, the second job would cause me to miss Sunday morning service.

When I got back in town that Sunday morning, I went home and went to bed. The church that I attended also held Sunday evening services. So after my nap, I started preparing to attend the Sunday evening service.

When I came to church that Sunday night, I felt the presence of the Lord in a way that I had never felt before. I know that this sounds strange, but it was as if God were saying to me, "I will do even more than this if you would let go of that second job and seek me."

That same night, I went into my former pastor's office and vowed before him not to accept another work assignment on my second job if it would cause me to miss another Sunday service. I am by no means advocating that a person should not work on Sundays. Instead, I am advocating that a person should not allow anything to get in his or her way when he or she is seeking to be filled with the Holy Ghost.

The missionary had been trying to get me to see that my first job that God had provided for me was sufficient for that stage of my life, and she did not want me to get sidetracked at such a crucial stage of my walk with Christ. From that day forward, after making that vow not to miss another Sunday service if it entailed going out of town for the second job, the Lord started blessing me more and more until the night of October 22, 1993, which was the night in which I was endowed with the Holy Spirit.

I thank God for the missionary who kept me on track. There is no doubt in my mind that I definitely would not have received the Holy Ghost without accepting and heeding her advice. She helped me to realize the fact that being endowed with the Holy Ghost is worth more than all the money in the world, even a billion dollars.

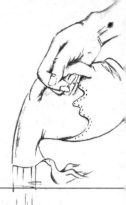

CHAPTER 6

Reverse Your Thirst

*Jesus stood and cried, saying, If any man thirst,
let him come unto me and drink.*
—John 7:37

Thirst is one of the strongest signals our bodies can send to us to let us know that our bodies are in need of hydration. Spiritually speaking, it is often said that there is a thirst in a man's soul that can only be quenched or satisfied by the things of God. It is also said that there is a void in a man's soul that can only be satisfied by the spirit of God, as discussed in chapter 5.

People may try to fill that void with many different things, but the satisfaction that they receive is only temporal. The soul is spiritual, so the void has to be filled with something spiritual. Unfortunately, many people allow themselves to be governed by the works of the flesh and spend the majority of their lives trying to quench that spiritual thirst with natural things. Soda, lemonade, and sweet tea all taste good going down, and they satisfy for the moment. After a while, though, you become thirsty again because what the body really needs is water.

When you try to quench a spiritual thirst with natural things, it is like a doctor who diagnoses his patient properly but then gives him the wrong medication, putting his patient in danger. This void or thirst will never be quenched with natural things, and the person must appropriately channel his or her desire from carnal things to spiritual things—things that can satisfy the thirst of the soul.

When people begin thirsting after spiritual things, they will recognize their need for something to quench their thirst and will realize that it will have to come from someone or something greater than themselves. They will begin to realize that their soul is parched and in need of spiritual water. They will humble themselves and admit that their souls are in need of a spiritual awakening.

Let's take a look at some of the natural thirst quenchers of the flesh that appear to be satisfying for the moment but afterward leave us in need of a spiritual thirst quencher. The Apostle Paul identifies these natural thirst quenchers and refers to them as the works of the flesh. He identifies these in Galatians 5:19–21 as the following: adultery, fornication, uncleanness, lasciviousness, idolatry, witchcraft, hatred, variance, emulations, wrath, strife, seditions, heresies, envy, murder, drunkenness, and revellings. It is likely that an unsaved person will find him- or herself engaged in one or more of these natural thirst quenchers.

Adultery
A man or woman breaking his or her wedding vows in order to have sexual relations with a third party

Fornication
Sex before marriage or any type of lewd sexual behavior, which includes adultery, sex with animals, and homosexuality

Uncleanness
Anything that defiles, bringing you into a state of defilement before God. This could include but is not limited to profanity, hatred, drugs, alcohol, tobacco, and unlawful sex

Lasciviousness
Shameless conduct with no boundaries, which may include one's sexual conduct and other sensual pleasures

Idolatry
To worship, love, or adore a person, place, or thing more than
God, having God take second place or replacing Him altogether

Witchcraft
Magic, sorcery, or divination and being associated
with palm readers, fortune tellers, and the like

Hatred
The fruit of jealousy; extreme resentment or dislike for a person or thing

Variance
To war against or cause contention, opposing that which is right

Emulations
Excelling at the expense of others or disregarding others to exalt oneself

Wrath
The result, fruit, or product of anger as it
manifests through one's sinful nature

Strife
Conflict; an ungodly dispute between two parties

Seditions
Ungodly divisions, groups, or cliques

Heresies
Ungodly divisions, groups, or cliques with the mission of opposing God

Envy
Jealously elevated to the highest extreme

Murder
The act of taking a life; to kill or destroy

Drunkenness
*The state of intoxication caused by drugs, alcohol, or anything
that will cause one not to think with a sober mind*

Revellings
*Wild parties or gatherings that come together for
an ungodly purpose—for example, orgies*

Unfortunately, Paul goes on to state that "they which do such things shall not inherit the kingdom of God." This may seem devastating and like it is the end of the line for those who find themselves doing these things, but this is not the case.

Jesus once again has provided a way to escape such a fate. The Apostle Peter writes in 2 Peter 3:9, "The Lord is not slack concerning his promise, as some men count slackness; but is long suffering to us-ward, not willing that any should perish, but that all should come to repentance."

The good news is that if you find yourself driving down the road to destruction, you don't have to keep going down that road. Up ahead there is a sign that says "U-Turn Permitted." Those who turn around don't have to run into that dead-end street called Destruction. Jesus, the greatest prophet in the history of earth, who came on the scene many years before Paul's letter to the Galatians, had the solution to this problem. Paul had the diagnosis, but Jesus has the medicine.

JESUS, THE SPIRITUAL THIRST QUENCHER

It can be proven through the scriptures that the water that Jesus offers as an alternative to fleshly desires is that of the Holy Spirit.

In John 7:37–39, Jesus says, "If any man thirst, let him come unto me, and drink. He that believeth on me, as the scripture hath said, out of his belly shall flow rivers of living water."

The Apostle John, who no doubt was following Jesus when He spoke this word of truth, convincingly and with strong emphasis states in verse 39, "But this spake he of the Spirit, which they that believe on him should receive: for the Holy Ghost was not yet given."

John makes known the fact that the rivers of living water that Jesus spoke of refers to the Holy Ghost. It is interesting that Jesus refers to the Holy Ghost as living water. This can be interpreted as water that makes one alive as well as leads to eternal life. Through his son, Jesus Christ, God is the giver of the Holy Spirit. Since Jesus is alive, everything that Jesus offers is alive. After all, Jesus is the source of life. The waters of ungodly fleshly desires, however, could be referred to as dead water because they lead us to eternal damnation and will not give us eternal life.

Historians claim that Jesus spoke these words during one of the popular feasts of the Jews, the Feast of Tabernacles. At the end of such a feast, it was customary for the priest to take a golden vial and fill it with water from the pool of Shalom and pour it out on the altar, which was the high point of this joyous occasion. The Jews— who ultimately rejected Christ—enjoyed going through fleshly rituals that brought happiness to the flesh but could never satisfy the soul. The same thing is happening in our society today. People are thirsting for something, but they really don't know what it is.

If a person has not met and made Jesus Christ their personal savior, they may be unknowingly trying to quench their spiritual thirst with natural or carnal things. Many people feel satisfied with making a lot of money, obtaining power and status, having a well-rounded social life, pursuing education, or traveling all over the world. All of these things are fine, but after a person attains these things, the satisfaction he or she may feel is short-lived. It may last for a season, and then the thirst will return.

How do we drink the water that Jesus gives? The word "drink" means to take in, ingest, swallow, or receive. When we drink a glass of water, that water is only beneficial to us if it goes inside our body. We can pour water on the outside, such as on our face. We may obtain some relief from doing this, but we only receive ultimate satisfaction when we get that water on the inside. Drinking the water that Jesus offers can be looked upon as receiving the gift of the Holy Ghost. John the Baptist spoke these words in reference to Jesus in Matthew 3:11: "I indeed baptize you with water unto repentance: but He that cometh after me is mightier than I, whose shoes I am not worthy to bear: He shall baptize you with the Holy Ghost, and with fire."

When we earnestly ask God to fill or endow us with the Holy Spirit, we are making our claim to God that we are thirsty and in need of a spiritual drink.

In John 4:6, Jesus was tired from his journey, so He sat on top of Jacob's well. Then along came a woman from Samaria to the well to draw water. When she saw Jesus sitting on top of the well, they had a conversation about thirst. Jesus told the woman, "Give me something to drink."

Because he was in the flesh, Jesus had a natural need that He wanted the woman to help Him with. The woman, who was not in the Spirit, had a spiritual need that only Jesus could help her with.

When Jesus asked the woman for a drink, right away, she began to make excuses. Let's look at the three excuses the woman gave Jesus.

"The Jews have no dealings with the Samaritans."

This woman of Samaria thought that Jesus would have nothing to do with her because the Jews had no dealings with the Samaritans. When a person does not have a relationship with God, it is not uncommon to feel alienated and to believe that God will have nothing to do with you.

"Sir, you don't have anything to draw with."
This woman of Samaria did not have the proper
means to draw water from the well. Similarly,
some of us do not know where we should start,
and we may not have the first clue of how to get
our spiritual thirst quenched.

"The well is deep." The woman of Samaria did
not see any possible way she could access the water.
Likewise, it may seem like it is impossible for us to
be endowed with the Holy Spirit, and the promise
may seem far beyond our reach.

This woman of Samaria realized her insufficiencies and
ultimately did not think that Jesus would have anything to do
with her, so in turn, she began to make excuses of why she could
not give Jesus water to drink. This is also true of us. When we sin,
we often feel inadequate, and we may believe that Jesus would have
nothing to do with us. This woman no doubt was thinking negative
thoughts about not having the proper means to give Jesus a drink.

When we are asking God to endow us with the Holy Spirit, we
cannot focus on all of the have-nots; instead, our focus should be
on Jesus, who can give us everything. The woman was focusing
on how deep the well was, which made it seem impossible to get
the water. When we are thirsting for God's living water, we must
go to all extremes. We must do whatever it takes to get our thirst
quenched.

Jesus tells the woman in the gospel according to John 4:10, "If
thou knewest the gift of God, and who it is that saith to thee, Give
me to drink; thou wouldest have asked of him, and he would have
given thee living water." One of the reasons that many people have
not yet received the gift of the Holy Ghost is that many people don't
know that the gift even exists.

People know the Holy Ghost as the third person of the Godhead, but they do not know Him as one who is able to take up residence in their souls. When we reverse our thirst by turning away from the natural and starting to yearn for the spiritual, we put ourselves in a position to be endowed with the Holy Spirit. This cannot be achieved until we know the gift and believe that God wants us to have the Gift.

The woman also did not know the man at the well who asked her for a drink. Jesus is the one who gives the Holy Spirit, and it is impossible to receive the gift without knowing Him. After we reverse our thirst, we have to do all that we can to develop a personal relationship with God.

Having a personal relationship with God allows us to receive not only the Holy Spirit but also any other gift that God intends for us to have. When we reverse our thirst, we prove to God that we have forsaken or given up the natural in order to receive the spiritual. After we have prepared to become converted and serve the Lord—after we have turned our life around from a lifestyle of sin to a lifestyle that pleases God—then there is nothing left to do but to ask for his heavenly gift.

Jesus told the woman at the well in verse 10 that if she had known about the gift of God, she would have asked, and He would have given her living water. It seems as if the woman had missed her opportunity, but after Jesus spoke with the woman, she perceived that He was someone great. This prompted the woman to make her request. In the gospel according to John 4:15, "The woman saith unto him, Sir, give me this water, that I thirst not, neither come hither to draw."

Jesus was trying to prepare the woman to receive the heavenly gift by telling her in verse 16 "Go call thy husband." Jesus knew that the woman had previously had five husbands and that the man she was with at that moment was not her husband. Jesus, knowing that the man she was presently with was not her husband, was hoping that she would acknowledge her wrongdoings and ask for forgiveness. These natural things in the woman's life needed to be addressed before she could ask Jesus for anything spiritual. Jesus wasted no time in directing her to these things. If we attend to the things that are hindering us from making a reversal in our lives and put away the natural to make room for the spiritual, we will never be dissatisfied with what Jesus has to offer. You will never be left with the feeling of an unquenched thirst.

A man once owned a 1969 Buick 225. The body of this car was in immaculate shape, and the engine ran superbly. There was a problem with the transmission, however, that would only allow the car to operate in drive. The owner of the car would drive and park the car in a way that he would not get pinned in because he knew that he could not back the car up. The man soon became weary of this inconvenience but could not afford to get the car fixed. The man decided to take the car to the junkyard and take whatever money that he could get for the car because he was badly in need. The owner of the car explained that the car would only go forward in drive and that he could not afford to get the car fixed.

The owner of the junkyard was amazed at the immaculate condition of the body of the car and wondered why anyone would bring a car with a body that well maintained into the junkyard. The owner of the car explained that the car would only go forward in drive and that he could not afford to get the car fixed. The owner of the junkyard offered the man $500; he knew that the car would be worth the money spent because it could be saved.

The owner of the car agreed to the offer, and as soon as the transaction was made, the owner of the junkyard took the car to the transmission shop. He discovered that the only thing the car needed was a new reverse gear. The new reverse gear was installed, and the car was spared from demolition.

Many of us are like that car. We are headed forward to destruction with no means to turn around, but Jesus stepped in and paid the price to save us from destruction and then ordered us to make a reverse. The only way that we can get to new spiritual heights and attain all that Jesus has for us is to reverse our thirst and let Jesus quench our parched and thirsty souls with the water of the Holy Spirit. If you choose to do this, you will never thirst again.

CHAPTER 7

I'm into Something, and I Can't Get Loose

Set your affection on things above, not on things on the earth.
For ye are dead, and your life is hid with Christ in God.
—Col. 3:2–3

When you are preoccupied with something and you become so indulged to the point of no return, you can say, *"I'm into something, and I can't get loose."*

When the Apostle Paul wrote to the Church at Colosse, he was writing to believers who had a *newfound faith*. The Apostle Paul's task was to get the members of the Colossian Church to elevate their lifestyles. He invited them to take a step up from their former lifestyle to a new life with Christ. The Apostle Paul also wanted them to know that when you become saved, the things that matter most in your life begin to take second place to the life that God has planned out for you. Therefore, your desires take a backseat, and your life becomes hidden in Christ.

I don't want you to misinterpret this. The Apostle Paul is not asking us to forget about our goals, dreams, or desires that we may have. Instead, he is asking us to reprioritize the things in our lives, making heavenly or spiritual things first on our list. We cannot make it into heaven if we become consumed with worldly things and allow those things to take precedence over the things of God.

The Christian's life is a life that is withdrawn from the world and becomes hidden. It is concealed in a place of security where only Christ has access. It is laid up far out of reach of our enemies. So then, a person who is converted and changes his or her lifestyle is like a hidden treasure that is tucked away from the world and is at Christ's disposal at any time.

I feel the need to explain the title of this chapter, "I'm Into Something, and I Can't Get Loose." Here the word "can't" does not mean the inability to do a certain thing. Instead the word "can't" means having no desire to do something. Therefore, we can interpret the title to mean "I'm into something, and I don't want to get loose."

Before my conversion I lived a life filled with defeats. Don't get me wrong—we had it better than a lot of families, and I would not change any events of my life if I had the power to. Because I was the oldest child in my family, I wanted to set a good example; however, I fell short.

In my life, I was an underachiever. If life were a game of sports, I would say that I was on the team that was losing. I was unable to go out and help my team win because I was on the bench. There were players better than me out there on the field. I was a zero, and without God in my life, I was kind of just going along in life. I was unable to sense any changes that I could make to improve my life. My personal defeats ranged from being mediocre in school to having epilepsy manifest in my body.

I considered myself to be a good person. Growing up I was fortunate to have good parents and a family that was intact. I was the oldest of four children. Four years after I was born, my mother gave birth again. This time she gave birth to twins unexpectedly. My mother stopped working in order to stay home and raise us. My father worked long hours and was the sole breadwinner. Two years later, my mother gave birth again. Even though there were four of us kids in total, ours was a small family compared to others.

My grandmother came from out of town to live with us and

help my mother take care of us, and she never went back. My parents raised us the best they could. I used to hear my father say, "Children don't come with an instruction manual."

My parents were members of a church, and I was christened as a baby. Early on, we never went to church much except for those special days, such as Palm Sunday, Easter, and Christmas. My mother and father knew the importance of being in church. As the years progressed, we began to attend church more and more.

Early on, God started showing me that I needed Him. Around the age of twelve, I was riding my bike through the alley, and as I turned the corner, I was hit by an oncoming car that knocked me six feet in the air. I escaped with only bruises. When I returned home with my twisted bike, I came into the house and explained to everyone what had happened.

My parents realized that this was an act of God's protection, but my grandmother was very determined that we needed to do more than just acknowledge this act. She took me down on my knees in prayer and made me thank God out loud for His protection and safekeeping. This time the prayer was different than the usual prayer we would pray on our knees before turning in for the night. When I began praying, I started to cry and as a result of this, I made my first commitment to God.

I began reading my Bible every day, and sometimes God would even allow me to see visions of the second coming of Jesus Christ. Unfortunately, this commitment was short-lived as peer pressure and being a teenager took first priority.

When I was sixteen, I became a member of the usher board. At this point, it would be safe to say that I had a commitment to the church and to the usher board, rather than a true commitment to Jesus Christ.

There was an older man who lived down the street. He was a faithful churchgoer. He invited all of the small children and teenagers on our street to Vacation Bible School. I took him up on this offer, as did a couple of my friends who lived on my street. After

Vacation Bible School ended, I decided to continue attending that church. I attended Friday night services as well as Sunday morning services. I even helped out by singing in the choir. I confessed that Jesus was my Savior and that I wanted to be saved from my sins, but once again this commitment to Christ was short-lived as sports, secular music, and girls took precedence in my life.

As a teenager, I started drinking alcohol and experimenting with drugs. This seemed to be the thing that most teens were doing as peer pressure once again set in. In 1978, when I was a sophomore in high school, I bumped my head while lifting weights in the school weight room. Later that night I had a seizure. I recall going to bed and waking up in the ambulance. The doctors thought that the seizure was caused from the bump on my head. Nevertheless, I was diagnosed with epilepsy, and the doctors stated that I would have to take medication for the rest of my life. I was prescribed 300 mg of Dilantin and 60 mg of Phenobarbital to be taken daily. After taking the medication for many years, I told my mother that I was not sure I needed to continue taking the medication, so my mother suggested that we make an appointment to take a new test to determine if I truly needed it.

When we entered the doctor's office, the doctor stated that he wanted to run two separate tests—one while I was awake and one while I was asleep. I passed the test when I was awake with flying colors. The test concluded that there was no seizure activity in my brain while I was awake.

The second test that I took while asleep came out different. The needle that was monitoring my brain activity went violently up and down on the page, showing seizure activity in my brain while I was asleep. The doctor concluded that any time I was asleep, I was susceptible to having a seizure, and therefore there was no way that I could get off of the medication. Instead I would have to take this medication for the rest of my life.

This was a big blow to me. The medication was giving me gum disease, and I could not get any worthwhile jobs because the Phenobarbital showed up in my blood as a barbiturate used in downers, so I was unable to pass a drug screen. Because of this, I continued to be an underachiever. While I was away at college, I had another seizure. This second seizure confirmed that this sickness was something that I would have to deal with for the rest of my life.

In 1983 I met a young lady at a cookout that my father had invited me to. She was very attractive and seemed to be very nice. She had a smooth, youthful complexion and a beautiful smile. Shortly after we met, we began dating. We dated for approximately two years before getting married in 1985 and relocated to Los Angeles, California. My wife loved being away and the new life that we had begun together, but I knew deep down inside that Los Angeles was not the place that I wanted to raise a family. In 1986 we moved back to Chicago, the place that we both knew as home to begin our family and to be close to both sets of parents. By 1990 my wife and I had found fairly decent employment, and we also had added two children to our family, Darryl and Ashley.

MY FIRST VICTORY

Wednesday, May 29, 1991, was a day that would change my life forever. I went to work just like any other day. At the time, I was employed as a truck driver working for a beverage company.

This particular day my load required two men, so I was assigned a helper to ride along with me in the truck. The helpers that my company used were not employees of my company but were pooled out of a day-labor service. I had had the opportunity to ride with many different people by this time, but the person I rode with on this particular day was different from any other individual I had ridden with in the past. God put this gentleman in my path in order that he might share the gospel with me.

When we were together, he asked me, "Do you know Jesus as your personal savior?" This was a question that I had heard before, so I simply answered, "I go to church." I was not ready for his next question. He then asked, "If you were to die today, where would you spend eternity?"

I had to be honest. I admitted to the gentleman—and myself—that I would not spend eternity with God in heaven because of the lifestyle I was living. After the gentleman asked that question, something strange happened.

A deep conviction came upon me, and I heard a voice saying, "Today may be your last chance." The gentleman offered to call his wife to lead me through the sinner's prayer, but I kept making excuses. Finally, though, I yielded to God's invitation. He called his wife, and she prayed with me over the phone. My sins were forgiven, and that day I started my new life in Christ.

The following Sunday, I attended the church that I had been a member of for so many years, but when I attended this particular Sunday, I felt an uneasiness that I had never experienced before. It seemed as if I no longer had anything in common with the people I had gone to church with for so many years, and deep down inside, I knew that this was no longer the place for me.

THE JOURNEY TO SPIRITUAL EMPOWERMENT

I had made many commitments to God in the past. They had all been short-lived, but this was the real deal. I truly repented of my sins and asked God to come into my life. This time I felt closer to God than I ever had at any other times in my life.

The search for a new church home was not easy. In fact, it proved to be dangerous. Little did I know that Satan would try to put roadblocks in my path to try to keep me from attaining what God had planned for my life. These roadblocks were secular music and a false sense of spiritual empowerment. If Satan had succeeded, he would have stopped me from coming into the full knowledge of Jesus Christ.

Let us look at the first roadblock of *secular music*. One day, that same gentleman who had introduced me to Christ came over to my apartment. Little did I know that I was about to make one of the biggest decisions of my life.

I was a music lover. I listened to all types of rock and roll, jazz, and R&B artists. I know some who are reading this will disagree and see nothing wrong with listening to secular music, but this day I would have to choose between Jesus and my secular music. Please allow me for just a bit to go into detail so that you can capture the intensity of this decision.

I started out at the age of seven or eight listening to my father and mother's records. I listened to all of the music of the '60s and '70s. In the early '70s, I started buying and collecting my own music, often asking my parents for money to go down the street to the record shop.

By the time I reached the age of thirteen, my appetite for music changed. I started listening to a harder form of music that further alienated me from Jesus Christ.

It was now 1991. I had been married for six years, and we had been living in this apartment for five years. By this time, my music collection, which consisted of albums, VHS tapes, and compact discs, was now worth about $3,000. When that gentleman came over to my apartment, he noticed this music collection and told me that listening to that kind of music would be contrary to my new walk with Christ.

At first I disagreed. I said, "There is nothing wrong with listening to music." His next question would knock me off my feet. He said, "Do the lyrics of these songs line up with what you are trying to achieve in your newfound salvation?"

I had to be truthful to God and myself, so my answer was no. He then replied, "Why keep this music in the house, then? It will only later prove to be a temptation." I then made the choice to not listen to this music, but I was not ready to get rid of it altogether. After the gentleman left, God started convicting me about the worldly music in my house.

The next time the gentleman came over, he showed me a scripture that is found in Acts 19:18–19: "And many that believed came, and confessed, and shewed their deeds. Many of them also which used curious arts brought their books together, and burned them before all men: and they counted the price of them, and found it fifty thousand pieces of silver." I believed that my music collection fell under the category of curious arts, and I knew that I had to make a decision, which turned out to be one of the hardest decisions of my life.

Would I choose Jesus, or would I allow Satan to deceive me into holding on to this worldly possession? I know that people have different things that they do not want to part with when they make the decision to serve God, and secular music was mine. I had done a lot of things in my unsaved life—drinking, smoking, doing drugs—but nothing was as hard as this.

I decided to reach out to a cousin of mine. We had grown up together, and we shared the same taste in music. I informed him about the positive change that I had made in my life, and I told him that I was discarding my secular music collection. I invited him to come over and take away the entire collection.

Evidently he thought my new walk with Christ was a hoax as he didn't show up in the one-week time span that I gave him. Over this time I thought to myself that this music collection should not be able to have control over anyone else in the fashion that it had controlled me.

A few weeks later, I made the decision to part with my secular music. I called the same gentleman who had been influential in witnessing to me and leading me to Christ, and we went to the store with my entire music collection in my trunk and backseat.

I did not want another person to be bound by this music collection like I had been, so I made the decision to do away with it for good. I went to a nearby store and purchased some lighter fluid. I then took my entire music collection to a nearby vacant lot.

There I piled my entire collection up, poured on the lighter fluid, and set it all on fire.

I cried because I had given up so much and would never be able to listen to this music again. Looking back at it now, I realize that it was not me who was crying. Instead, it was the old me. I was now denying my old self, along with all of my worldly ambitions.

I hope what I say next is not misinterpreted as being an illusion, but during the very same moment in which I was crying, I heard God speak to me in an audible voice for the first time. On the inside, I heard, "I will bless you." This all happened on a Saturday evening.

The next day when I went to church, I felt God in a way that I had never felt Him before. I had now crossed the first hurdle on the journey to spiritual empowerment.

The next hurdle that Satan tried to throw in my path was a false sense of spiritual empowerment. Although I did not know much about salvation, I began going around to different churches with a childhood friend of mine. In the process of going to these different churches, I kept hearing about being filled with the Holy Ghost with the evidence of speaking in tongues.

I had previously heard and experienced the baptism in water but never this. On this particular Sunday, the minister made a plea for anyone who wanted to receive the gift of the Holy Ghost to come to the altar. I went to the altar with great expectation. There were a lot of people at the altar, and for the first time, I started hearing people speaking in tongues. At the time I believed that they were speaking in tongues as a result of having received the Holy Ghost.

It seemed as if everyone who came to the altar immediately began speaking in tongues. My mind was open. If this was what God wanted for me, I certainly was not going to do anything to stop it. At the same time, I did not want to do anything of my own accord. I wanted God to be in control.

Although I was glad to be at the altar, I was not compelled to speak in tongues on my own. Instead I believed that if God had ordained this experience to happen to me, I would not have to do anything of my own accord.

One of the gentlemen who was working with the people who were at the altar approached me and asked me what was wrong. I responded, "Nothing!"

He then asked me, "Why aren't you speaking?"

I replied, "I don't want to do or say anything on my own."

He then said, "The Holy Spirit will give you the utterance, but you have to speak it out of your own mouth." The gentleman then pressed on my stomach and told me to speak. I started speaking, saying what I heard other people saying. I felt happy. As far as I was concerned, I had received the Holy Ghost.

I could not wait to get home to give my wife the great news. When I told her everything that had happened, I expected her to be happy and to rejoice with me. Instead, I saw that concern was written all over her face. She was not happy at all.

My wife had been converted about four years before me, and she had had more experience being a Christian than I had. My wife wanted me to tell her everything that had happened. When I went over the story again before her, she was not enthused.

I felt betrayed. This was supposed to be the most exciting time of my life. Instead my excitement was snuffed out by my wife's feelings of concern and worry.

My wife wanted me to talk with our children's babysitter, who was the ultimate example of Christianity. I had just gotten saved and was still on the search for a church home, but my wife was already a member of the same church that this outstanding Christian woman, our children's babysitter, belonged to.

I told the story again of what happened to me at the altar that day to the woman. When she heard it, she knew that this had not been a true, authentic Holy Ghost experience. This outstanding Christian woman was filled with wisdom, and she set out not to discourage me. She told me, "God has more for you." I thought that these people—the Christian woman and my wife—were not there and had no right to tell me that I had not received the Holy Ghost.

As all of these events began to unfold, my wife grew more and more concerned. She set up a time for me to meet with her pastor, which would prove to be the meeting of meetings.

I continued to spend time with the gentleman who had witnessed to me. We had Bible study together, and on occasion, I even visited his church. His church reminded me a lot of my wife's church, which I had visited a few times before I had been converted.

Even though I had not long been converted and did not know all of the church protocol, I strongly believed that a man should not be a member of a church separate from his wife and family. So I stopped going to my childhood friend's church where I had had that questionable experience. My search for a new church home was narrowed down to two—the church of the gentleman who had witnessed to me and led me to Christ and the church that my wife belonged to.

I went to church with the gentleman on the Friday night leading up to my Sunday afternoon meeting with the pastor of my wife's church. I enjoyed the service very much, and the gentleman pressed me to join. But I wondered, why should I join this church when my wife and family were elsewhere? My decision was now pending on the outcome of my meeting with my wife's pastor.

When I stepped into the office of my wife's pastor that Sunday evening, he asked me to go through the story again of what had happened to me when I was at the altar of my childhood friend's church. When I finished telling him the story about receiving the Holy Ghost, to my surprise, he not one time disputed my claim. Instead he celebrated my newfound salvation. I thought that I finally had someone on my side.

My wife's pastor was a man of wisdom, and he knew that if he could get me inside the church, I would get a chance to truly experience the Holy Ghost. So wisely he did not dispute my claim, which would have turned me away. I was very pleased with the outcome of the meeting. I told my wife's pastor that just because I had previously received the Holy Ghost, this did not mean that I would stop seeking God.

My wife's pastor knew that my experience was not authentic, but he wisely replied, "Good, son. That is the thing to do." On that same night after staying over and experiencing the Sunday evening service, I decided to join the church, and my wife's pastor became my own.

MY FIRST MIRACLE

One Sunday, after becoming a member of my new church, my pastor preached a message about God's divine prescription. The message focused on God's supernatural ability to heal our sicknesses if we only had faith to believe. After hearing this message, I was encouraged to trust in my faith.

It was 1991, and I had now been taking the medication for my seizures since 1978. The doctors said that I would have to take the medication for the rest of my life. This was the perfect time to exercise my faith in God.

I stopped taking my medicine, 300 mg of Dilantin and 60 mg of Phenobarbital. My wife thought I was losing my mind, and she was concerned because she didn't want to see anything happen to me. She was happy that I had decided to exercise my faith, but she thought that I was taking it a bit too far when I ceased to take my medicine.

My parents and the rest of my family expressed their concern. They also explained that they were happy with the strides that I was making in my newfound faith but thought that I was taking it a bit too far. My wife pleaded with me over and over again out of love for me to take my medicine.

I had been on medication for thirteen years at this point. Because I had abruptly stopped taking it, I started having withdrawals. I was laid off from my job, and all I wanted to do was sleep and lay around. It was even a challenge for me to attend church services, but I was not to be discouraged. I continued to believe that God was able to heal me from epilepsy.

One Monday afternoon the withdrawals got worse. It was about four o'clock in the evening, and I decided to take a nap. When I woke up, it was about seven o'clock. A strong urge came over me to read my Bible, so I got up and went to the kitchen table and opened it up.

I had not long been converted and had no idea what I was going to read, so I just opened up the Bible and started reading. When I opened the Bible, it was at the place of Mark 11:22–23. Little did I know that I was about to experience God speaking to me for the second time along with my first miracle.

Mark 11:22, 23 states, "And Jesus answering saith unto them, Have faith in God. For verily I say unto you, That whosoever shall say unto this mountain, Be thou removed, and be thou cast into the sea; and shall not doubt in his heart, but shall believe that those things which he saith shall come to pass; he shall have whatever he saith."

Immediately after I concluded reading that scripture, I heard God's voice for the second time in my life. God spoke to me while I sat at my kitchen table. He told me, "You are healed." His voice was loud but quiet at the same time. His voice was on the outside but on the inside at the same time.

God had given me my confirmation that my body had been healed. I could not wait to tell my wife what had just happened. When I told her about it, she was happy but cautious and suggested that I share this experience with our pastor.

When I told our pastor about what had transpired that Monday night, he perceived that God had worked a miracle in my life. On the following Sunday morning, the pastor allowed me to share my testimony on the church's radio broadcast. When I recited the story of how God had healed me, the entire congregation was overjoyed as the spirit of God came in our midst.

This was the best thing that had ever happened to me in my entire life. I was on the mountaintop and did not want to come down.

A HUMBLING EXPERIENCE

I made it a point to attend every service. The services were dynamic. The freestyle worship and the way that the musicians played and the choir sang filled any void left by the absence of secular music in my life.

As weeks went by, I started watching different people during the services, especially those who had openly professed that they had been filled with the Holy Ghost.

When the Holy Ghost was manifested in the services, I could not help but notice how the congregation was affected. As a new convert, I could not sense when the Holy Spirit's presence would come in the church, but I went off of everyone else's reactions.

I began to be disappointed because I was not experiencing the same thing as the other people in the congregation. I was careful not to do anything on my own, and I definitely wasn't going to force anything, but something was not right.

After attending several of the services, I came to the realization that I did not have the same gift that the other people in the congregation had. I liked what I was seeing so much, however, that I was willing to do anything to get what these other people had.

In one of the Sunday evening services, I humbled myself. After seeing the many different manifestations and administrations of the Holy Spirit, I had to admit that I did not have what I had thought I had at all. I told the church openly that evening, "I am going to seek God until I get the same gift that they had." From that night forward, I started asking God to fill me with the Holy Ghost, but the road to my spiritual empowerment would not be easy.

It was now 1993, about two years and five months since the day of my conversion. This period was filled with ups and downs, highs and lows, peaks and valleys.

Although you do not have to necessarily be in a church service to be filled with the Holy Ghost, many of the congregants of my new church made the claim that they had been endowed or filled with the Holy Ghost during revivals or in a church service. I now know that God can fill you with the Holy Ghost at any place and at any time of His choosing.

When a revival approached, I would get excited over the potential of receiving the Holy Ghost, but when I did not and the revival was over, I would get discouraged. Two and a half years of this spiritual roller-coaster ride was enough. It was time to put all of my focus and energy toward being filled with the Holy Ghost.

My pastor was a man of great faith who fasted and prayed often. I learned the art of fasting from my pastor as I witnessed how the power of God manifested in his life. I told my pastor that I was going to fast for forty-eight hours every week until God filled me with the Holy Ghost.

My mind was made up. I was focused and determined. I did not care how long it was going to take. If I had to fast for ten weeks or two years, I was determined to fast until I was endowed or filled with the Holy Ghost.

A NIGHT TO REMEMBER

It was Friday, October 22, 1993. This was the fourth or fifth week into my weekly fast. This particular week I had started the fast on Thursday, October 21, and I was scheduled to break the fast Saturday, October 23. I kept my mind on the Holy Spirit every day, and this day was no different as I anticipated the Friday night service.

When I arrived at church that night, I was a bit early, and I had the chance to sit in the pews and read some Bible scriptures. When

I opened my Bible, I felt an urge to read every scripture I could find concerning the Holy Ghost.

It was time for service to start, and I felt a strong urge to stand on my feet and lift my hands and praise God. From the moment I lifted my hands in the air, I could feel the Holy Spirit overshadowing me on the outside. The entire congregation and I were praising God.

This night was different. This night belonged to me. I hoped that this would be the night that God would fill me with the Holy Ghost. The more I raised my hands, the more I could feel the presence of God overshadowing me. This was the closest that I had ever felt to God.

The atmosphere of the service changed dramatically. By this time, my pastor knew that this was going to be an unusual service. They worked with me to help me stay in that supernatural spiritual place that I had never experienced before and kept me encouraged as we waited on God.

I had never experienced the power of the Holy Ghost like I was experiencing it this night. The more I praised God, the more I could feel His power. I ended up on the floor and under the pews under the power of the Holy Ghost.

While I was on the floor, I thought, *If I can just make it back on my feet, I can lift my hands to praise God once again.* Every time I would rise to my feet and raise my hands to the Lord, the same thing would happen over and over again.

I can remember the missionary of chapter 5 coming over to me while I was on the floor. I did not know it at the time, but now I realize that at that particular moment, God gave her the spiritual eye to see the Holy Ghost alongside me as He waited for the right opportunity to go inside of my soul. Revelation 3:20 says, "Behold, I stand at the door, and knock; if any man hear my voice, and open the door, I will come in to him, and will sup with him, and he with me."

The Holy Ghost was overshadowing me on the outside, but it was up to me to give up all and invite Him on the inside.

I started speaking in tongues as the Holy Ghost began to make His entrance. I was not doing anything on my own, unlike what I had experienced at my childhood friend's church earlier. The Holy Ghost had taken complete control of me. I was into something and couldn't get loose.

I would speak in tongues awhile and then stop. I was so full of joy that the Holy Ghost had taken control of my tongue, but this was not enough. I wanted the Holy Ghost to go down in my innermost being.

Two of the ministers of the church were sent over to me to pick me up from the floor and bring me to the altar. I did not have any control of my body. Once I was at the altar, I said within myself, "This is the place I want to be."

While at the altar I dropped down on my knees, submitting myself to God. I started clapping my hands and praising God as loudly as I could. While I was on my knees clapping my hands, there was something deep down on the inside of me that wanted the Holy Ghost more than anything else in the entire world.

Since Jesus is the one who baptizes with the Holy Ghost, I had an overwhelming strong urge that came from the inside to call the name of Jesus as loudly as I could. While I was on my knees at the altar, I leaned back and called Jesus's name as loudly as I could from down in my belly. The two and a half years of fasting, praying, and waiting for God at the altar were all contained within that one call for Jesus.

At that very instant, the Holy Ghost went down into my innermost being and started speaking out of me in unknown tongues. I had no control of my speech and could no longer say anything in English. It was coming from down in my belly. John 7:38 says, "He that believeth on me, as the scripture hath said, out of his belly shall flow rivers of living water." The Holy Ghost had gone down into my soul and had complete control of my speech and body in such a way that after the service was over, I was unable to gather my things and drive my car home.

One of the ministers at the church, a great friend of mine, drove me home that night. While riding home in his car, the radio was on. There was a man on the radio who called out the name of Jesus over the airwaves. When I heard Jesus's name, it connected with the Holy Ghost in my soul, and again, I started speaking in tongues uncontrollably.

When we got to my home and he pulled in the driveway, I was still under the Holy Spirit's influence. I was unable to get out of the car, so he helped me out. On the way in the house, I saw the neighbors looking out of the window. They thought that I was drunk. I was, but I was drunk with the new wine of the Holy Spirit.

When I got in the house, I did not even bathe or shower. I just lay in the bed, basking in the presence of the Lord. Many times during the night, as my wife lay by my side, I could feel the Holy Ghost in my belly. I woke up several times during the night speaking in tongues.

I can feel the Holy Ghost on the inside even now as I write about this account that took place years ago. This was the greatest thing that had happened to me in my entire life. The Holy Ghost engulfed me and had complete control over my mind, body, and spirit. This was truly a night to remember and one to be cherished for the rest of my natural life.

CHAPTER 8
Finally Filled

*For John truly baptized with water, but ye shall be
baptized with the Holy Ghost not many days hence.*
—Acts 1:5

Early one Saturday morning in the spring of 1994, not long after
that glorious night of October 22, 1993, the Holy Ghost woke
me and began ministering to me. He revealed to me that what He
had done in my life and in the lives of other believers was the work
that God the Father sent Him to do.

Jesus said that the Holy Ghost would reprove the world of
sin. Before my conversion, the Holy Ghost proved to me that I
was a sinner. Like a lawyer would do when he is building a case,
the Holy Ghost laid out all of the evidence that I was a sinner and
left me with the decision to repent of my sins. When a person
has not yet been converted, the Holy Ghost will allow them to
feel the guilt from their sin, but on the other hand, after a person
is converted, the Holy Ghost consoles that individual. The Holy
Ghost will convict you now (before conversion) and comfort you
later (after conversion).

The Holy Ghost also made Jesus become real in my life. Jesus
was no longer some character I had read about in the Bible. The
Holy Ghost helped me to realize that Jesus was alive and working
in my life.

The Holy Ghost tuned me to the right channel to get in contact with God as my prayer life began to flourish. The Holy Ghost helped me talk to God when I did not know what to say or how to pray.

There was no doubt in my mind that Jesus had been crucified to pay the debts from our sins, nor that he had been buried and risen from the grave and is now seated at the right hand of the Father in heaven. Through the ministry of the Holy Ghost, there wasn't any doubt in my mind that Jesus had lived a holy and righteous life and was accepted by the Father. Even though Satan is our enemy and is constantly warring against us, the Holy Ghost helps us to realize that Satan was defeated by Jesus, and his future has been determined.

My life took a turn for the better after being filled with the Holy Ghost. It was now much easier for me to focus on the things pertaining to God. The word of God became easier to understand. Scriptures that I had previously misunderstood or not understood at all were suddenly opened up to me. It was easier to fast, pray, and supplicate before God.

The temptations that I faced seemed to roll off like water, as the Holy Ghost was my new aid. It became a bit easier to deal with death as the Holy Ghost let me know that none of us are here to stay and that He will accompany us to the grave and comfort us when we lose loved ones.

In addition, it took almost no effort for me to make it to every church service. I wanted to be in the presence of the Holy Ghost as much as God would permit. It also became easier for me to talk to people about Christ, and in those instances, I experienced boldness. From time to time, God allowed me to speak in tongues, and it would happen spontaneously. I did not have to do anything on my own.

Scriptures would pop in my head, and I would experience a strong urge to write them down immediately. On one occasion, after writing down several scriptures, they seemed to be arranged in sermon format after I wrote them down.

In the same year, 1994, the Holy Ghost called me into the gospel ministry. When I answered the call, the Holy Ghost promised me that He would help me and be with me. I often can feel the Holy Ghost on the inside of my soul. When this happens, I get a burst of encouragement to continue on.

The Holy Ghost ministers to me when I face those especially tough situations in my life and encourages me. He explains to me that He will never leave me, but I have the duty of making sure that I never leave Him.

The relationship that I have with Jesus through the Holy Ghost is still fresh as He continues to teach, lead, and guide me. I pray that the will of God be done in my life as I strive each and every day to please Him.

By no means have I arrived. There is still plenty of work to be done, but I am convinced that the Holy Ghost is the man for the job. Thank God that I am finally filled!

BONUS

Holy Ghost—Quick Study Guide

The Holy Ghost worked and manifested Himself throughout the Old Testament and continues to work today in this dispensation of the church age. If allowed, He will also take up residence in the soul of the believer. The following is a quick study guide of some of the work that the Holy Ghost has done or will do.

A. The Holy Ghost is referred to by Jesus in the Gospel according to John as He, Him, or Himself nineteen times in chapters 14–16. This illustrates that the Holy Ghost is virile and masculine, such as Jesus and the Father.
   John 14:16, John 14:17, John 14:26, John 15:26, John 16:7–8, John 16:13–14

B. The Holy Ghost had a part in creating the earth and man.
   Gen. 1:2, Gen. 1:26

C. The Holy Ghost empowered Bezaleel with wisdom, knowledge, and workmanship to build a tabernacle for the Lord.
   Exod. 31:3

D. The Holy Ghost put Balaam in a trance and empowered him to prophesy to Balak.
   Num. 24

E. The Holy Ghost empowered Saul and David to become the kings of Israel.
   1 Sam. 10:6, 1 Sam. 16:13

F. The Holy Ghost filled John the Baptist in Elizabeth's womb.
   Luke 1:15

G. The Holy Ghost oversaw the conception of Jesus in Mary's womb.
   Luke 1:35

H. The Holy Ghost empowered Jesus for ministry in the Jordan River.
   Matt. 3:16, Mark 1:10, John 1:32

I. The Holy Ghost desires to dwell on the inside of believers, but He will not abide if your body or temple is unclean.
   1 Cor. 6:19, 2 Cor. 6:16, Luke 4:1

J. The Holy Ghost raised Jesus from the dead and will also raise believers from the dead in the resurrection.
   Rom. 1:4, Rom. 8:11

K. The Holy Ghost will convince sinners that they need salvation, prove to the world that Jesus was righteous, and make known the fact that Satan has already been judged and awaits eternal destruction.
   John 16:7–11

L. The Holy Ghost anoints and appoints his preachers.
   Acts 20:28, 1 Cor. 2:4

M. The Holy Ghost fills believers who ask for it both individually and corporately, when believers are gathered together as a body.
   Luke 11:13, Acts 2:4

N. The Holy Ghost regenerates the converted sinner and gives her or him the nature of God.
   Titus 3:5

O. The Holy Ghost gives us revelation of God's plans and purposes.
   Luke 2:26

P. The Holy Ghost gives you power to execute the game plan that God has for your life.
   Acts 1:8

Notes

_____

_____

_____

_____

_____

_____

_____

_____

_____

_____

_____

_____

_____

_____

_____

_____

_____

_____

_____

Notes

_____

_____

_____

_____

_____

_____

_____

_____

_____

_____

_____

_____

_____

_____

_____

_____

_____

_____

Notes

Notes

Notes

_____

_____

_____

_____

_____

_____

_____

_____

_____

_____

_____

_____

_____

_____

_____

_____

_____

_____

_____

Notes

Notes

_____

_____

_____

_____

_____

_____

_____

_____

_____

_____

_____

_____

_____

_____

_____

_____

_____

_____

_____

_____

Notes

Notes

Notes

_____

_____

_____

_____

_____

_____

_____

_____

_____

_____

_____

_____

_____

_____

_____

_____

_____

_____

_____

Notes

_____

_____

_____

_____

_____

_____

_____

_____

_____

_____

_____

_____

_____

_____

_____

_____

_____

_____

_____

Notes

_____

_____

_____

_____

_____

_____

_____

_____

_____

_____

_____

_____

_____

_____

_____

_____

_____

_____

_____

_____

Notes

Notes

Notes

_____

_____

_____

_____

_____

_____

_____

_____

_____

_____

_____

_____

_____

_____

_____

_____

_____

_____

_____

Notes

_____

_____

_____

_____

_____

_____

_____

_____

_____

_____

_____

_____

_____

_____

_____

_____

_____

_____

_____

Notes

_____

_____

_____

_____

_____

_____

_____

_____

_____

_____

_____

_____

_____

_____

_____

_____

_____

_____

_____

_____

_____

Notes

Notes

Notes

_____

_____

_____

_____

_____

_____

_____

_____

_____

_____

_____

_____

_____

_____

_____

_____

_____

_____

_____

_____

Notes

_____

_____

_____

_____

_____

_____

_____

_____

_____

_____

_____

_____

_____

_____

_____

_____

_____

_____

_____

Notes

Notes

Notes

_____

_____

_____

_____

_____

_____

_____

_____

_____

_____

_____

_____

_____

_____

_____

_____

_____

_____

_____

Notes

_____

_____

_____

_____

_____

_____

_____

_____

_____

_____

_____

_____

_____

_____

_____

_____

_____

_____

_____

_____

_____

Printed in the United States
by Bookmasters

Printed in the United States
By Bookmasters